discovermore

Economics in Your Community

Goods and Services

Sloane Wilden

Britannica Educational Publishing
IN ASSOCIATION WITH
THE ROSEN PUBLISHING GROUP

Published in 2024 by The Rosen Publishing Group, Inc.
2544 Clinton Street, Buffalo, NY 14224

Editor: Brianna Propis
Book Design: Michael Flynn

Photo Credits: Cover Branislav Nenin/Shutterstock.com; (series background) Dai Yim/Shutterstock.com; p. 4 MK photograp55/Shutterstock.com; pp. 5, 24 BearFotos/Shutterstock.com; p. 6 Artazum/Shutterstock.com; p. 7 Ground Picture/Shutterstock.com; p. 8 Guitar phtographer/Shutterstock.com; p. 9 Serg64/Shutterstock.com; p. 10 Valentin Valkov/Shutterstock.com; p. 11 Oaklizm/Shutterstock.com; p. 12 Animaflora PicsStock.com/Shutterstock.com; p. 13 The Drop Zone/Shutterstock.com; p. 15 (top) Goncharov_Artem/Shutterstock.com; p. 15 (bottom) Basilico Studio Stock/Shutterstock.com; p. 16 hurricanehank/Shutterstock.com; p. 17 zhu difeng/Shutterstock.com; p. 18 WindNight/Shutterstock.com; p. 19 (top) Africa Studio/Shutterstock.com; p. 19 (bottom) Ann in the uk/Shutterstock.com; p. 20 Sura Nualpradid/Shutterstock.com; p. 21 Alex Kolokythas Photography/Shutterstock.com; p. 23 Wachiwit/Shutterstock.com; p. 25 Guillem de Balanzo/Shutterstock.com; p. 27 (top) Pixel-Shot/Shutterstock.com; p. 27 (bottom) Riccardo Arata/Shutterstock.com; p. 28 fornStudio/Shutterstock.com; p. 29 Andrey_Popov/Shutterstock.com.

Library of Congress Cataloging-in-Publication Data

Names: Wilden, Sloane, author.
Title: Goods and services / Sloane Wilden.
Description: [Chicago, IL] : Britannica Educational Publishing, [2024] | Series: Discover more: economics in your community | Includes bibliographical references and index.
Identifiers: LCCN 2023030227 | ISBN 9781641900270 (library binding) | ISBN 9781641900263 (paperback) | ISBN 9781641900287 (ebook)
Subjects: LCSH: Economics--Juvenile literature. | Supply and demand--Juvenile literature.
Classification: LCC HB183 .W54 2024 | DDC 330--dc23/eng/20230815
LC record available at https://lccn.loc.gov/2023030227

Manufactured in the United States of America

Some of the images in this book illustrate individuals who are models. The depictions do not imply actual situations or events.

CPSIA Compliance Information: Batch #CWBRIT24. For further information contact Rosen Publishing at 1-800-237-9932.

Contents

Goods and Services 101

The study of the economy and the consumption of goods and services is called economics. Economists look at how people create wealth, how they use it, and how different people get different amounts of it. Wealth is not just money. Wealth comes from the production of goods and services, which people buy with money.

Goods can include electronic devices, such as cell phones, as well as the electricity needed for them to operate.

If someone does a job for payment, like serving food at a restaurant, they're providing a service.

Goods are items **consumers** buy, such as food, clothing, electronic devices, shoes, and furniture. Some goods are manufactured, such as computers and cars. Other goods are grown, such as fruits and vegetables. A service is an action that a person does for someone else, such as swimming lessons, dental work, car washing, serving food, and booking vacations. Goods and services are conducted by either people or machines.

WORD WISE

A PERSON WHO BUYS GOODS OR SERVICES IS CALLED A CONSUMER. IF A PRODUCER BUYS THEIR OWN PRODUCTS, OR SOMEONE ELSE'S, THEY'RE ALSO CONSUMERS!

Consumer and Capital Goods

Consumer and capital are the two specific types of goods. Consumer goods are the final products purchased by consumers, such as soap, toys, and pillows. Capital goods are the materials used to produce other goods and services. The cloth used to make a pillow and the plastic used to make a toy are just a couple of examples of capital goods.

Consumer goods, such as a bed or clothing, can probably be found in your own room!

Fruits and vegetables are goods that can be grown locally or out-of-state. Some fruits can only be grown during certain seasons, which can affect the taste.

Some goods are grown or produced locally. For example, farmers might grow crops and distribute them in their community to local grocery stores. Trees from a local forest might be used to build homes. Different states and countries can even send goods and services around the world.

Consider This

Do you buy your clothing and books online or in a store? Do you know where they're being made or being shipped from?

The Production Process

The process of production involves the creation of goods and services. There are three major factors in production:

Land: Land can refer to a large farm, manufacturing center, or a tiny workshop.

Labor: The people who are paid to produce goods and services.

Capital: The resources—such as the tools, factories, and offices—that are used to make the goods and services.

Farmers grow crops and raise animals using the land around them. The animals they raise, such as cows, are used to produce milk, food, clothing, and more.

Land can also be used to grow natural resources, such as corn, which is used to make various foods, corn oil, livestock feed, biofuel, and chemicals. Even the husks of corn are used for industrial purposes.

Goods are either manufactured or grown. Many goods are made from natural resources, such as wood. Wood is used to manufacture paper, books, doors, tables, and more. Human resources are the people who provide services.

Consider This

What other products do you use on a daily basis?
Can you think of what natural resources may have been used to make them?

There are many factors that determine if a good or service can be produced in a certain area. One factor is the resources that are available. For example, a country that does not have access to oil will not be able to produce gasoline. But a country that has rich soil can produce many **crops**.

Kansas is known to have rich soil and excellent farmland. Kansas is a leading producer of wheat, sorghum, corn, soybeans, and sunflowers in the United States.

Highly skilled workers are needed to manufacture complex pieces of equipment. A company or country with highly skilled workers can make products and sell those to other countries.

The skills of those producing goods and services are also a factor. If an area has skilled workers, the community can make products using complicated machines.

WORD WISE

CROPS ARE PLANTS THAT ARE GROWN AND HARVESTED AS FOOD FOR CONSUMPTION AND PROFIT.

Earth's Goods

Earth provides many natural resources—such as air, water, plants, animals, rocks, and minerals—that people can use to create goods. Some resources are renewable, which means they can be replaced or grown back. For example, plants are renewable resources. Farmers plant new crops each season.

Solar power can be used to create electricity. It can even be used to power a house!

Deforestation is the mass removal of trees for use of wood or land. Forests will not survive if new trees are not planted to replace the ones that are cut down.

Non-renewable resources cannot be replaced or they take a very long time to be replaced. Fossil fuels, such as coal, oil, and natural gas, are non-renewable natural resources.

Even renewable resources must be managed carefully. Wood is a natural resource, but if too many trees are cut down, we could run out of wood and damage the environment.

Consider This

Fossil fuels are naturally formed from the remains of plants and animals. It takes millions and millions of years for them to form. Does that make them renewable or non-renewable? Why is it important to protect these resources?

Industrial Contributions

A group of businesses that makes or sells similar products or offers similar services is known as an industry, which is a key part of the economy. There are several main groups of industries, including agriculture, mining, manufacturing, and community services.

The agriculture industry is everything related to farming. Mining refers to the removal of metals and other materials from the earth. Humans mine metals to make tools, jewelry, and many other goods. Manufacturing industries make things that people buy. Manufacturers take resources such as metal, wood, and cloth and turn them into products to sell.

Service industries provide services to customers. Media and entertainment is one example of a service industry. Movie theatres provide spaces for guests to watch new movies, and the popcorn and sodas offered are more attached goods available.

The demand for industrial goods is impacted by the demand for consumer goods.

compare and contrast

Think of the many different products and services you and your family might use. Which ones can be grouped into similar industries? Which ones are from different industries?

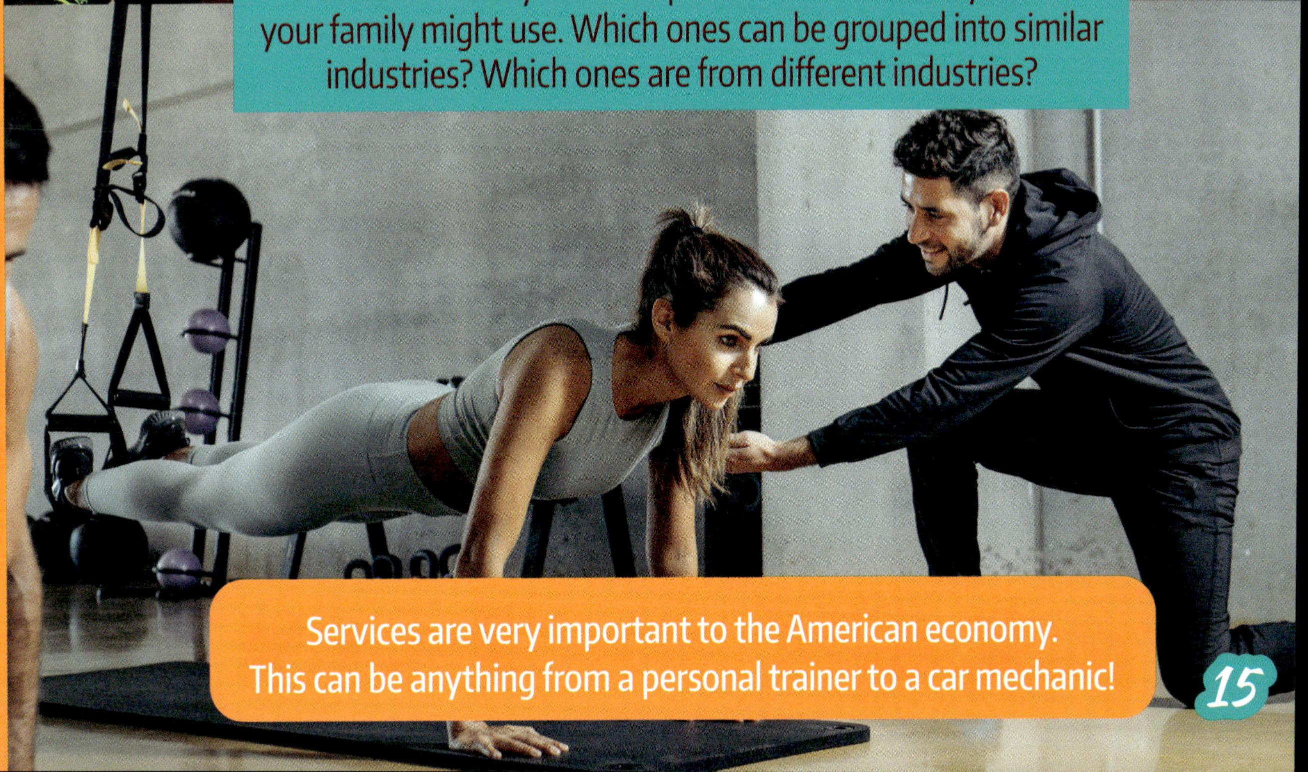

Services are very important to the American economy. This can be anything from a personal trainer to a car mechanic!

Meeting Demand

Supply and demand determine the price of products. Supply is the amount of something available to consumers. Demand is how much consumers want something.

Producers often raise the price of a product, such as a hot new toy on the market, if it's selling well.

A product not selling well will likely have its price decreased, as producers want to encourage people to buy it.

When the demand for something is high and supply is low, producers raise the price to make more money. This is especially true for items made from limited resources. Scarcity occurs when there are not enough resources to fulfill a need. If there is a large supply of a product that not many consumers are buying, producers will lower its price to encourage people to buy it.

Consider This

If you purchase a lot of goods and services from foreign countries, how might that affect the American economy? If you purchased them from people making or selling them locally, how might that affect the American economy?

Demand is the desire for people to buy a product they either need or want. A need is something a person must have to survive, such as food, water, and shelter. A want is something someone would like but is not necessary for survival. Bikes and video games are wants. People can survive without them. Both goods and services can be either a need or a want.

People, animals, and plants all need water to survive. It's free in many parts of the world. In others, water is harder to find. Still, some people spend money on bottled water every day.

compare and contrast

Make a list of the items in your home. Which of them do you need to survive, and which are ones you may enjoy but could survive without?

A dessert after dinner may taste delicious, but we don't need sweet treats to survive!

Supplying the Public

An industry works because of the way producers and consumers supply one another, forming a market. A market is any place in which people buy or sell goods and services. A market can be a physical place, like a department store or a car dealership, or it can refer to the group of people who all want or need the same types of items.

Distribution means to spread a good or service throughout the market so that many people can buy it. It can be simple or complex depending on whether a good or service is going across town or across the world.

Oranges are packaged in cartons or boxes to ensure they're not damaged while in transport.

Food transported on a vehicle is known as cargo.

Goods and services rely on transportation systems. A truck brings oranges from a farm to a nearby grocery store. If those oranges are going from Florida to New York, a variety of transportation vehicles might need to move them to their destination via a **supply chain**. Trains, planes, cars, or even a ship might carry them.

WORD WISE

A SUPPLY CHAIN IS THE SERIES OF ACTIONS FOR A PRODUCT TO BE SENT FROM PRODUCER TO CONSUMER.

Creation of Goods

Before a **product** can be sold, the idea needs to be planned, created, and tested. Product development is the process of bringing a product to market. New products are developed all the time.

We live in a global economy, which means that markets around the world are connected. When a product is developed, parts for that product can come from all over the world.

Just because a product says it was "Made in America" doesn't mean the entire product was manufactured in the United States. For example, a car might have electronics that come from one country, tires from a second country, and a frame from a third. These parts are first purchased by the company making the product, then used in an assembly line to finalize the items.

Consider This

In a global economy, how does each country's contribution to a specific product support numerous industries and companies?

Labels found on many items, such as clothing, tell you where it was made.

WORD WISE

A PRODUCT CAN BE ANY ITEM MANUFACTURED AND SOLD FOR CONSUMERS. NEW PRODUCTS ARE OFTEN TESTED BY MANUFACTURERS. SOMETIMES THEY'RE TESTED IN FOCUS GROUPS, WHICH IS WHERE A COMPANY CAN SHOW THEIR NEW ITEMS TO CONSUMERS WHO PROVIDE FEEDBACK.

Industry Competition

When numerous producers are selling the same product or service, competition will arise between them. Sellers use many actions to get buyers to purchase their products. These actions can include sales and special offers designed to lure consumers toward buying one product over another. When more products are available, consumers get to choose what they want. Competition also keeps prices in check. A company can charge as much money as they want for their product if there are no other choices for the consumer. But consumers might still decide the product is too expensive and choose to not purchase it.

If a person is looking to buy a new piece of furniture, they might compare the prices offered at different stores and choose the less expensive one.

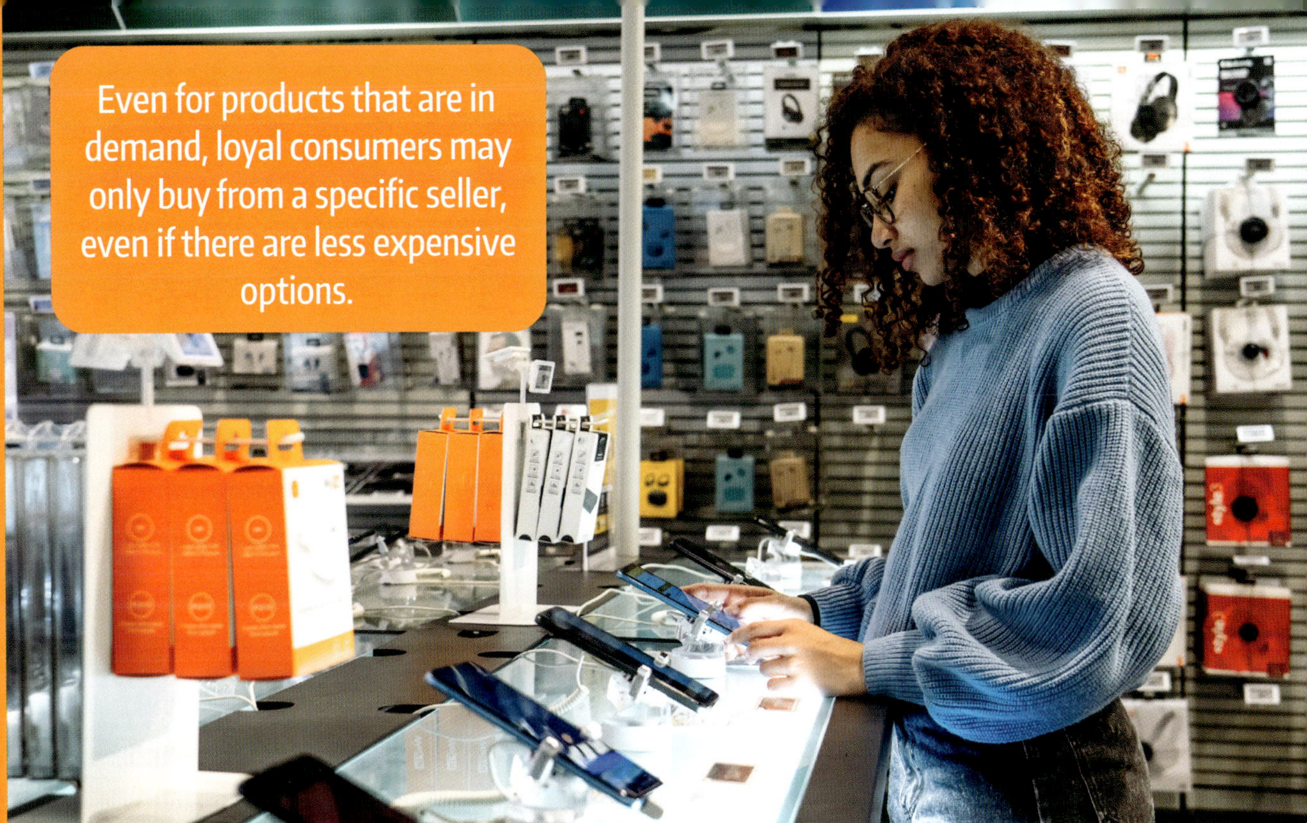

Even for products that are in demand, loyal consumers may only buy from a specific seller, even if there are less expensive options.

If one product is better than another and a lot of consumers are buying it, the manufacturer of that product might raise its prices. That's because the product is in demand. A company making a similar product may lower their prices so more people will choose to buy that one over a more expensive one.

Consider This

How might product quality and consumer loyalty influence supply and demand?

Commerce Trade

The buying and selling of products and services is called trade, or commerce. People have traded since prehistoric times. Today, most countries take part in international trade, or trade across country borders.

Trade happens for several reasons. A country may need or want goods that they do not have. The country may not have the workforce or the resources to manufacture the goods themselves. A country may also trade for services when they do not have the time or the skills to provide those services.

Both people and countries want trade to benefit them. Families want to earn more money than they spend on goods and services. Countries try to import, or bring in, as many goods as they export, or sell.

When you buy a good or service with money, you're engaging with trade! You're trading your hard-earned money for a product you need or want.

compare and contrast

If one country imports and exports numerous goods, and another does not, how do you think their economies are affected? Will one economy be more prosperous, or thriving, than the other?

Machines and computers are Italy's largest export—making up over 16.2 percent!

The World's Economy

Goods and services are the power source for economies around the world. They provide jobs, which provide paychecks to families. The families in turn use their money to buy the goods and services they need and want. This **cycle** keeps a country's economy strong.

Goods and services create wealth, which means people can afford to do and buy more—creating a cycle for an economy to flourish.

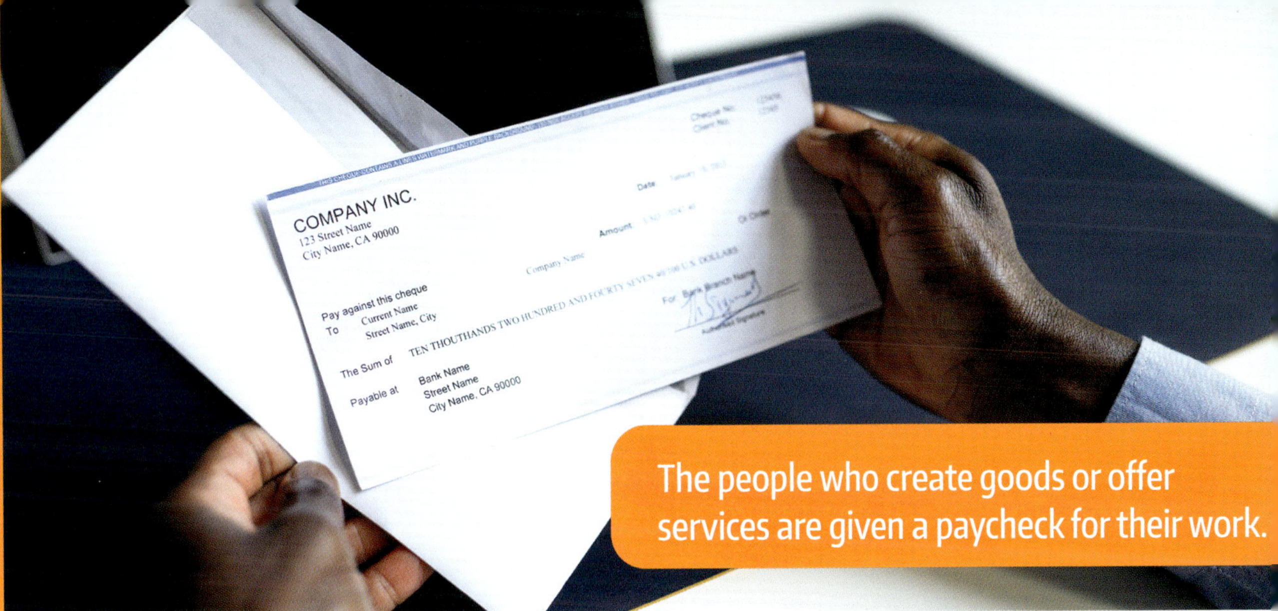

The people who create goods or offer services are given a paycheck for their work.

Not all countries have the people and materials that they need to produce the goods and services that they need and want. This leads to trade. The global economy depends on trade. It puts goods and services into the hands of those who need them but cannot get them in their own countries.

Goods and services help to create wealth, both for individuals and for countries. If a country has a strong economy, they can provide better resources for those living within it.

WORD WISE

A CYCLE IS A SEQUENCE OF EVENTS THAT REPEAT IN THE SAME ORDER REGULARLY.

Glossary

assembly The putting together of parts that make up a complete structure, machine, or unit of a machine.

customer One that buys a product or service.

distribute To divide among several or many.

economist A person who studies the economy.

export To carry or send abroad goods, especially for sale in another country.

import To bring goods into a country from another country, usually for selling.

international Involving two or more countries.

labor The services performed by workers for wages or payment.

market A meeting together of people to buy and sell goods or services.

natural resource Something that is found in nature (such as a mineral, waterpower source, or forest) that is valuable to humans.

production The act or process of creating a good or service.

profit Money that comes from selling a good or service, after the costs of produding the goods or service are deducted.

public Open to or shared by all.

scarcity Not having enough of something.

skilled Having a talent or ability.

sorghum One kind of Old World tropical grasses that look like corn and is used to make syrup, flour, animal feed, and other products.

wealth A great amount of money or possessions.

workforce The workers of a specific activity or business.

For More Information

Books

Flynn, Sarah Wassner. *Not-So-Common Cents: Super Duper Important Facts About Money You Can't Afford to Miss*. Washington, D.C.: National Geographic Kids, 2023.

Kishtainy, Niall. *The Economics Book: Big Ideas Simply Explained.* New York, NY: DK, 2018.

Lee, Kelly. *What Is Supply and Demand? Little Economists.* San Jose, CA: Econ for Kids, 2022.

Websites

Economics

jr.brainpop.com/socialstudies/economics/

Learn more about goods and services and needs and wants through informative videos and fun games.

Money and Finance, Supply and Demand

www.ducksters.com/money/economics.php

Money and the economy are further explained here.

Index